# I Wish I'd Paid Better Attention In Vacation Bible School

Mark B. Weaver

Illustrations by Ben Wade

WESTBOW
PRESS®
A DIVISION OF THOMAS NELSON
& ZONDERVAN

Copyright © 2014, 2018 Mark B. Weaver.

All rights reserved. No part of this book may be used or reproduced by any means, graphic, electronic, or mechanical, including photocopying, recording, taping or by any information storage retrieval system without the written permission of the author except in the case of brief quotations embodied in critical articles and reviews.

WestBow Press books may be ordered through booksellers or by contacting:

WestBow Press
A Division of Thomas Nelson & Zondervan
1663 Liberty Drive
Bloomington, IN 47403
www.westbowpress.com
1 (866) 928-1240

Because of the dynamic nature of the Internet, any web addresses or links contained in this book may have changed since publication and may no longer be valid. The views expressed in this work are solely those of the author and do not necessarily reflect the views of the publisher, and the publisher hereby disclaims any responsibility for them.

Unless otherwise indicated, Scripture quotations are from:
*The Holy Bible,* New International Version (NIV)
©1973, 1978, 1984, 2011 by Biblica, Inc.
Used by permission. All rights reserved worldwide.

Other Scripture quotations are from:
*The Holy Bible,* New King James Version (NKJV)
©1984 by Thomas Nelson, Inc.

*Italics* in Scripture quotations are the author's emphasis.

This is a work of fiction. All of the characters, names, incidents, organizations, and dialogue in this novel are either the products of the author's imagination or are used fictitiously.

ISBN: 978-1-9736-1589-7 (sc)
ISBN: 978-1-9736-1590-3 (hc)
ISBN: 978-1-9736-1591-0 (e)

Library of Congress Control Number: 2018902592

Print information available on the last page.

WestBow Press rev. date: 9/13/2018

This is a work of fiction. It is also the result of my reflection on several years of life and realizing that most of the things I've learned, I wish I'd learned in Vacation Bible School. The lessons were there, but the learning took a lifetime. I love the Bible stories in which Jesus is talking to the crowd in parables, and then later when He is alone with His disciples, they ask, "What in the world were You talking about?" For this reason, you will see two parts to each daily event—the imagined parable with various children and then how this applies to our relationship with a loving God. The book is set up to read each event as a devotional or just a reflection on how God works through everyday events to show how He loves us. May you not only enjoy this book, but may you also come to experience the love of God through the childlike faith He delights to find in you.

—Mark

# Contents

Didn't See This One Coming!
*Unmet Expectations* ............................................................... 1
Just Show Up!
*It Doesn't Matter How You Arrive* ........................................ 3
Don't Forget the Nap
*Who's It Really For?* .............................................................. 7
Red and Yellow, Black and White …
*We Ain't All Alike, Are We?* ................................................... 9
You're a Moon to Me
*Reflecting God's Love* ........................................................... 11
Lookin' and Findin'
*Discovering What God Has Created* ..................................... 15
Show and Tell
*Life Pictures* .......................................................................... 19
Grown Up Like a Child
*Maturity Isn't What We Think It Is* ....................................... 21
How Big?
*My Dad's Bigger than Your Dad* ............................................ 25
I Thought You Was My Friend
*Only Friends Can Betray You* ................................................ 27

Some Just Get It
  *Well, It Ain't Easy for Me* ...................................................... 31
Kool-Aid Mustaches and Broken Cookies
  *Or Dude, Loosen Up!* ............................................................ 35
Forgiving and Giving
  *Forgiveness* .......................................................................... 37
Gotcha!
  *No You Don't; I Got the Red Flag, Dude!* ............................... 41
Great Catch!
  *You Can't Play Pitch and Catch with Yourself* ........................ 45
Say What You Mean, Mean What You Say
  *The Truth Comes after the "But …"* ....................................... 47
WWMMD? (What Would Miss Marla Do?)
  *Close, but Wrong Question* .................................................... 51
Grace Isn't Just a Word
  *Grace Applied* ...................................................................... 55
Live with the End in Sight
  *It's Really Just the Beginning* ................................................. 59
Judging
  *Intentions vs. Actions* ............................................................ 63
Sliding Down the Banister of Life
  *Sometimes We Just Need a Push* ............................................. 67
Stand or Fall
  *Short of the Truth* ................................................................. 71
What If
  *What If What?* ..................................................................... 73
Singin' in the Key of Free
  *When Did I Stop Skipping?* ................................................... 77

Who Is That?
*Foreigner, Brother, Sister* ........................................................ 79
A Day in the Life of a Coke Bottle
*The Great Exchange* ................................................................. 83
Who Are You?
*Whose Are You?* ...................................................................... 87
The Stress of Uncertainty
*Finding the Unchanging* ......................................................... 91
What Kind of Soil?
*Amazing What Can Grow Through the Cracks* ..................... 95
The Battle
*Oh, Behave!* ............................................................................. 99
How High?
*Measuring Our Dreams* ......................................................... 103
Faith or Denial?
*Denial Often Masquerades as Faith* ..................................... 107
Which Is Better, Giving or Receiving?
*"Exchanging Gifts" Is an Oxymoron* ..................................... 109
Where Is Everybody Now?
*Love the Ones You're with Later, Too* .................................. 113

# Didn't See This One Coming!

## *Unmet Expectations*

It was my first day, and I was going to have things *my* way. I would do what I wanted, when I wanted, the way I wanted, regardless of what some ol' Vacation Bible School worker had to say.

Dude, I was there to play and have a good time.

So Buck, Eric, Ryan, and I were wrasslin' and shooting spitwads at the girls and the guy with the black horn-rimmed glasses, when all of a sudden Miss Marla hollered out, "Now children, let's all be quiet and say a prayer to get started."

Stop and be quiet? That wasn't my idea of having fun.

The rest of that first day, I pretty much sulked, caused trouble, and acted like a smart aleck.

Things really weren't going as I'd expected. I'd fully intended to have my way, which was my idea of fun.

By the end of the day, I'd started to resent the fact that I even had to be there.

Ryan, being the "ol' man" of our group, noticed my behavior and bad attitude. At the day's end, he asked me, "Did you like the Kool-Aid? The cookies? The games? The songs? The painting?"

Well, as I thought about it … yes, I liked all those things. *But I didn't get my way!*

## Expectations in the Way

Life. What are our expectations? It's funny how we allow our expectations to get in the way of living and enjoying what God has put right in front of us.

There's a saying in AA about how "unmet expectations lead to resentments." How freeing it can be when we surrender having our own way and instead allow God to lead.

How many times have I had unspoken expectations of others, judging their actions by what I think I would have done? We go through life judging others by their actions and ourselves by our good intentions.

I've sometimes allowed my expectations of myself and how my life should be to get in the way of simply living. May those expectations dissolve and yield into an expectancy of living in the present … in *His* presence.

# Just Show Up!
## *It Doesn't Matter How You Arrive*

Natasha rode to Vacation Bible School in a beater van and got out with at least fourteen more kids who were all from the neighborhood across the way.

Buck rode his bike with the sissy bars, banana seat, and lime green tires.

I thought Eric had walked, but he made his mom drop him off down the street so no one could see her beater of a car.

Ryan rolled out of a last-legs Dodge van driven by his mom—who was also our teacher, Miss Marla.

Emily was part of a car pool of kids whose moms took turns every day.

And Timmy rode in a Cadillac Escalade.

You know, as kids we observed all this—but once we were in the door, it really didn't matter how we got there. It was just that *we were there*.

# The Final Ride

How much time have we spent in pursuit of "rides"? Not just dollars spent on vehicles, but the whole materialistic, make-life-as-enjoyable-as-possible, first-class rides of this temporal world? How much time have we wasted in acquiring, or thinking about acquiring, and then maintaining all the stuff?

Someday I'll stand before my Abba Daddy with my buddies from my Vacation Bible School days. In that moment, I'll be fully aware that all my time that wasn't lived in His perfect will was for nothing.

In that day, we'll all have new rides—and we'll understand that what really matters is simply that we're *there with Him!*

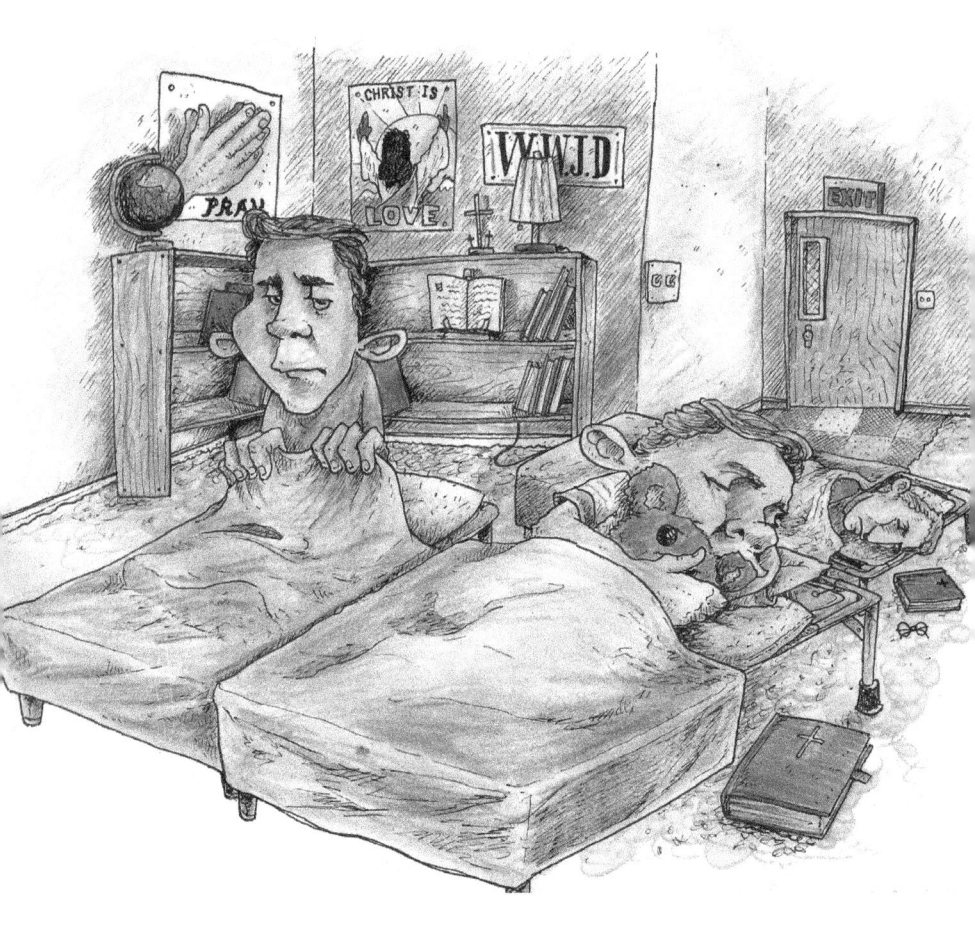

# Don't Forget the Nap

## *Who's It Really For?*

A nap? No way!

We were having such a blast, coloring, cutting, pasting, and eating the paste. *Now we gotta take a stinking nap!* I hated to slow down having all that fun, so I decided, *I will not sleep. Not going to do it.* What kind of fun was a nap?

Since I was forced to lie there anyway, I was the "worm in hot ashes" my dad would often say I was like. I tossed and turned. I sang, I talked. I pulled nearby pigtails and giggled.

Others might need rest—but I needed action!

The result?

By the end of the day, I was cranky, irritable, and incorrigible. I'd gone from fun to finished.

This meant (as I soon learned) that my friends would run the other way when they saw me coming. Even Miss Marla got an exasperated look on her face.

# Resting Is Trusting

It seems that some things don't change much. It's amazing how I still assume that the harder I work and the less sleep I get, the more I'll get done.

Yet constant striving and driving myself always led me to failure—failure to care, failure to love, failure to trust and live.

I can't live without rest. Period. Because resting is *trusting*.

Trusting is faith. Without faith, I can't please God.

May I trust Him and His design for my everyday life, resting in Him.

# Red and Yellow, Black and White

## We Ain't All Alike, Are We?

Eric—you could always spot him. I remember wondering why he wore long-sleeved flannel shirts and long pants on hundred-degree days. His scotch-taped glasses rode low on his always-runny nose, while he tried to edge out one word at a time.

Eric was the one who wouldn't let his mom drop him off at church because, as I found out later, he was ashamed of the old car she drove. That's not all he was afraid to show. If you rolled up his sleeves, you could see scars from where his dad had put out his cigarettes.

The first thing Eric would do when he got to Vacation Bible School was dive into the cookies (reserved for the rest of us, I was sure). I hated this selfish move. But Miss Marla would quickly go to him and help him with not only the cookies, but also a glass of milk or two. (That part I didn't mind, as long as he didn't drink my Kool-Aid!)

I would wonder: *Why such special treatment for him?* What had he done to deserve this attention?

Later in the week, some things would happen that would give me insight to the answers for my questions.

## Eyes to See

The Lord does not look at the things people look at. People look at the outward appearance, but the Lord looks at the heart (1 Samuel 16:7b).

We cannot see what God wants us to see in others when we are blinded by the prejudices we hide behind to shield us from those different than us. When we ask God to remove these 'protective' blinders, He first enables us to see the deep need we have for His love and then empowers us to love others just as they are.

*Lord, give me Your eyes to see in others not their obvious garments but the beautiful creation You've designed each of them to be. May I see the wounds that cry for Your healing, the shame that begs for Your cleansing.*

*May I love the ragamuffin that each of us is. And know that one day, You'll make all things right.*

# You're a Moon to Me
## *Reflecting God's Love*

It happened every day. Miss Marla would greet each of us with a Mary smile and Martha feet. She would hurry around getting stuff done, while always stopping to hug one of us.

She had a gift of making you think you were the only one in the room. Four kids could ask her four questions, and they all thought she was answering each of them personally.

She also had eyes in the back of her head. I never got away with anything. Whether I was giving Eric a mule bite or pulling Emily's pigtails, she would catch me, even without their protest. Secretly, I think I wanted her attention, because she had a way of correcting me and loving me at the same time.

Just like Jesus.

## Bringers of Light

Looking back on my life, I remember all the different people who brought light to me. Some were children, some were teachers, some were bosses, and others were just passing through.

Today, I understand that they weren't the light; they simply reflected light like the moon reflects sunlight.

We need light to see, and that light allows us to recognize God's love for us when it's reflected by other people.

I wonder what keeps us, as believers, from reflecting God's love. How easy it is to develop a sheath of selfishness that dulls our ability to reflect God's perfect light.

I pray that we can truly clothe ourselves in humility to reflect the perfect light of God's love to others, like Miss Marla did.

# Lookin and Findin

## Discovering What God Has Created

Enter Emily, a blond beauty—well, a beauty to everyone except Ryan and Timmy; to these six-year-olds, she's just a girl. Kinda yuck, though at least a cute yuck.

Ryan hollered out to get Emily's attention, but she stayed quiet.

Emily was often quiet with her mouth, but her eyes would speak a thousand words, leaving you to sift through their meaning to wonder what was truly going on inside her.

Ryan began to explain to Timmy that Emily was an artist. "Yeah, she draws real good. But when she's done, she has to explain what it is."

"Why's that?" Timmy asked.

"Cause she sees things that others don't see. One time she drew what looked exactly like a tree. When everyone said it was a beautiful tree, Emily said, 'It may look like a tree, but it's *pain*.'"

"Pain?" Timmy asked.

"Yeah," Ryan went on, "she said the tree was made by God, but some awful men made a cross out of it, and they tortured and killed Jesus on it. Pain."

"Wow," Timmy said. "She really is different!"

Emily was always discovering things that others just walked right on by.

Today, Emily sat quietly next to the boys, waving her crayons across the canvas of yellow construction paper. Ryan and Timmy occasionally stopped their futile attempts to color within the lines as they got lost in watching Emily work and smile.

Finishing, she stepped back to look at her picture. The landscape was dark, except for the round yellow sun emerging from the part of the construction paper Emily had left untouched.

Intrigued by this, Ryan said, "If I hadn't seen you do it, I never woulda guessed a girl coulda created that."

"You're silly," Emily responded. "I didn't create that … it was already there."

## Discovering What's Already There

"I have never started a poem yet," wrote Robert Frost, "whose end I knew. Writing a poem is discovering."

God is the Creator; we are not. God reveals His creation and His love for us through His Son, Jesus Christ.

I've always been amazed at how we, created people, give so much glory to things that we and other people "create." Even the greatest musical composers are only discoverers. God created sound and the ability of our ears to hear. He created each note, each beat, each rhythm, each melody line, and chord. All that the greatest or simplest composer ever accomplished was to discover what God had already created.

God created us to be discoverers. He designed us to seek—that is, to discover His great love for us. He created the beauty in each one of us and can lead us to discover the wonder in each other, red and yellow, black and white. Yes—to discover that everyone is *precious in His sight.*

Regardless of gifts or deficits, normal or weird, useful or useless, ugly or pretty, smart or dumb, loving or unloving ... He wants us all to discover Him in each other. But first, we must discover how much He loves *us*—opening the way for us to love others as ourselves.

# Show and Tell
## *Life Pictures*

"What are you doing with that silly bird?" asked Eric.

"Melody is my favorite pet in the whole world," Emily declared, holding up the birdcage. "I brought her today for show and tell."

Buck examined the cage more closely. "Where's the door?"

"Well it broke off one day, when I was trying to take care of Melody," Emily answered.

"Why doesn't that bird just fly away through the door?" Bubba asked. "Is he stupid?"

That got Emily upset.

Miss Marla intervened. "It's a *she*!" she said, correcting Bubba. "And Melody doesn't fly away because she knows Emily will take care of her."

Emily spoke up again. "Oh yeah, Melody flies out sometimes—but she always comes back."

# Alternate Insights

David once praised God with these words: "How priceless is your unfailing love, O God! *People take refuge in the shadow of your wings*" (Psalm 36:7).

Have you ever wanted to hide? I mean under the bed, as still as an opossum, quiet as a mouse? We all need a refuge at some time in our lives. Yet every form of refuge has a price.

Some of us may hide beneath the momentary mountain of relief that comes from abusing drugs. Some cocoon themselves in unhealthy relationships, thinking that by losing themselves in such a relationship, they'll be safe. Others hide behind excessive work, using constant achievement as a cloak to mask their own illusion of having to take care of themselves and their family with stuff instead of with their presence. Some even hide in doing good works, trying to cover over their deep-felt craving to be needed, desired, and loved.

If we hide anywhere other than beneath the shadow of His wings, we're not safe. We may feel safe for a moment, but as soon as our position changes, our deeply haunting fears are exposed. And our deepest fear is that of being unsafe.

So what's the price for freedom?

When I think of being free, I realize that I sense freedom only when I'm living within God's will for my life. This is the place where I know He's taking care of my every need.

Yet the price for my freedom wasn't free. No, I didn't pay for it; Jesus Christ paid for it with His life. Now He lives that life through me, allowing me to walk in true freedom.

Sure, I could flee from my cage—and at times I've chosen to do so. But sooner or later, I realize that my only real refuge and freedom will come from staying in His will.

# Grown Up Like a Child
## Maturity Isn't What We Think It Is

"Come on, Eric, can't you even tie your own shoes?" Bubba asked.

"I knew how to tie my own shoes when I was three," Eric boasted in reply. "My daddy taught me. I remember him telling me it was time to grow up."

None of us kids realized that Eric *had* to grow up. He was basically on his own. His mom worked two jobs; his dad, meanwhile, drew a disability check that kept him in beer money. He would be drunk by noon and mean by 12:01. So Eric spent most of his time outdoors.

Miss Marla would always greet Eric and then take him into the kitchen to wipe his nose and dirty ears. Often she would slip him a ham sandwich that no one would see. She seemed to have a radar for him; whatever needs he had, she would meet.

The other kids at times would notice this and call Eric a baby and say he needed to grow up and take care of himself. They probably said those things mostly because they were jealous of the attention Eric received.

Growing up was on all of our minds, even at ages five and six. The appealing idea of being independent was already taking root.

## Look at It Backward

There's a great contrast between being mature as a human being and being a mature Christian.

Our goal as parents is to teach our children to become independent of us. As a child grows up, a mark of maturity should be the ability to depend upon himself or herself.

The opposite is true for a mature Christian. The goal is to recognize and act upon our utter dependence upon Jesus Christ to bear fruit in our lives, for He tells us that apart from Him, we can do nothing. A branch cut off from the vine will not bear fruit. The branch depends totally upon the vine for its whole life.

I remember well many frustrating years trying to produce fruit on my own. Oh yes, I would ask God to bless what I was doing, but I wasn't asking Him *what* to do and then depending upon Him to work through me to produce His results.

My next step of maturity came when I realized more clearly my need to ask for His guidance and help, but at first I was still trying to get an expected result. I was close, but still frustrated—because things often didn't turn out the way I thought they should.

True maturity resulted when I let go of those expectations and started depending upon God's power and *His* results. He is God and I am not—so I had to learn to trust Him, since it was always His will that determined how things turned out.

Remember again the truth from Philippians 2:13—how God

is so much at work in us for *His* good pleasure. My job is to surrender and to allow Him to do this work and get the results.

How vain it was to think I knew what the outcome should be. I can't see the end; only He can.

# How Big?

## *My Dad's Bigger than Your Dad*

It all started when Eric lost the paper-wad basketball game to Buck. Like the rest of humankind, Eric hated to lose, so he told Buck that his dad was bigger than Buck's dad.

Buck replied, "My dad can touch the ceiling."

Eric replied, "My daddy can touch the roof!"

Not to be outdone, Buck said, "My daddy can stand on top of the whole building."

Eric continued the verbal wrestling match: "My dad could get to the moon!"

Then Miss Marla waded into the fray. "Boys, I think both of your daddies are great. But let me tell you that each of you has the *same* Father."

The boys were instantly stunned. *Huh?*

"Each of you has a *heavenly Father*," Miss Marla went on, "a Father who made you and loves you so much that He sent His only Son, Jesus, to show His love for you. When you accept His love and the forgiveness that Jesus offers for all the bad things you've done, then you, too, become a son of the Father in heaven.

"Your heavenly Father made and loves each of you the same,

regardless of your successes or failures. And your Father in heaven is the One who created everything you can see and even the things you cannot see. There's no one bigger than your heavenly Dad!"

As she spoke, I could sense the truth: I need a Daddy that big!

## Large and in Charge

I love the verse in the book of Job when God addresses Job and asks, "Where were you when I laid the earth's foundation?" (Job 38:4). How often I get too big for my britches, thinking I'm large and in charge! How often, too, I can see what others accomplish and feel so small and incapable.

In either situation, my sin is to start comparing myself to others, looking for ways to justify my goodness or my sinfulness. I'll start to think I'm not as bad as someone else or start wishing I somehow could be as good as someone else. Both represent a wrong thought process and a wrong view.

Yes, I need a Daddy who's big. I need to know He's there wherever I am. I need to know that His strength is made perfect in my weakness. I need to be aware that my goodness is only filthy rags in comparison to His goodness.

As I continue to walk with Him, I know that it is He who lives His life out through me to accomplish the destiny He desires for me.

I can truly rest in knowing that *He is large* and *He's in charge*—of everything.

# I Thought You Was My Friend
## *Only Friends Can Betray You*

Wow, what a day we were having! Keith and I had started out being a terror team by making fun of everyone we saw. He and I would move around the room taking turns quipping about speech impediments, booger noses, short britches, baggy shirts, and whatever else other kids were saddled with through no fault of their own. Boy, we were causing a ruckus. We went on and on, till finally Miss Marla called us out and told us to play nice.

Well, Keith took her threat as real, but I pretty much just ignored it and got to making fun of Keith instead of the others. I knew his secrets and tender spots, and before long, he was crying and telling me I really wasn't his friend anymore and to just leave him alone!

Unfortunately, by this time I'd already insulted everyone else, as well as alienating my best friend there.

Miss Marla, having compassion on me after recognizing what I'd lost by my own hand, took me and held me. She told me I was someone Jesus loves and forgives and then extended her hand to Keith, so he could do the same.

From bitter … to sweet. Forgiveness.

## Betrayal

Have you ever been betrayed by an enemy? No; you expect them to slander, slap, and stab you. Because that's what an enemy is supposed to do. But a *friend?*

If you're reading this—or putting it another way, if you're breathing—then you've been betrayed, and you've also betrayed someone else. Whether it was a slip of a secret, a word that should have been left unsaid, an attack on the other person's character, or throwing someone under the bus instead of taking rightful blame, betrayal is an experience we all know. We betray; and we're betrayed.

I can envision Jesus after His arrest, there in the courtyard, with Peter in the distance looking on—just after he had vehemently denied even knowing this Jesus. Here was the same Peter who Jesus had said He would build His church upon. It was this same Peter who had boasted that all the others might fall away, but never him!

Jesus would feel the emotional pain foretold in the prophetic words in David's psalm: "If an enemy were insulting me, I could endure it; if a foe were rising against me, I could hide. But it is you, a man like myself, my companion, my close friend" (Psalm 55:12–13).

So what did Jesus do? Peter betrayed Jesus by denying Him three times; Jesus later restored him in a manner that allowed Peter to affirm his love for Jesus three times (see their conversation in John 21:15–17). This allowed Jesus to go deep with the restoration.

Three times Peter would claim and reclaim his love for the Friend who had given up His life for him.

So what are we to do when we betray or are betrayed? We're to ask forgiveness *and* forgive—through the power of the One who loves us, Jesus Christ.

# Some Just Get It
## Well, It Ain't Easy for Me

Ryan was just one of those kids—easygoing, never in a rush. And humble—not thinking less of himself, just thinking of himself less.

Ryan was even friends with Eric, someone who everyone else had the ability not only to turn away from but also to use as the manure to grow their own self-esteem.

Ryan would be the last in line, the first going to sleep at naptime, and always present in the moment. Yet it seemed, as I look back, that he knew some things we didn't.

He was old for his age, yet he could play with the best of us, and all the while staying sensitive to others.

Once I was pulling Keisha's cornrows, and Ryan spoke up. "Mark, would you want her pulling your hair?" What a different perspective!

I apologized to Keisha on the spot. Now, apologizing was *not* something that came naturally to me. If I got away with something, that made me proud; that was natural for me. Admitting I was wrong was tough.

Later that day, A. J. smacked me, and Ryan saw it. He came

to my defense and asked A. J. the same question he'd asked me earlier. It cuts both ways, I guess.

I often wondered why Ryan seemed to have it all together. Miss Marla was his mom, but even she would later tell me that Ryan was born different. He seemed to encourage her far more often than she encouraged him.

Ryan *got* it—he realized young that his Daddy in heaven was in love with him. He always lived with one eye toward heaven, knowing that this kind of farsightedness would always clarify any shortsightedness he might experience here on earth.

## Like Who?

It's true; some things just come easier to some people.

How easy it is to look at others and think, *They **get** it*. And we often think this isn't fair. We tell ourselves, *I have to try so much harder than they do,* or *I can't ever be like them.*

Well, we can never *be* them; being them is *their* job. But when we see Christlikeness in others, we can be encouraged to know that He does indeed give Himself to us, so we can be like *Him*.

The fruit of the Spirit is Jesus Christ in us. It's not our part to produce this fruit—but only to bear it and give it away.

Our "this ain't easy for me" part is a reality we'll often experience as we surrender to Him, allowing Him to live out His life through us.

We can learn, as Ryan did, that *striving* is His part—and *surrender* is ours.

# Kool-Aid Mustaches and Broken Cookies

## *Or Dude, Loosen Up!*

Miss Marla hollered out the door, "Everybody come in! Time for snacks!"

Well, she didn't have to holler twice!

Buck was the first one up the hill, the first in line, and the first with Kool-Aid stains on his face and shirt.

Man, could Buck eat! He was all elbows and lips, shoveling cookies in his freckled face. And he could not have cared less what anyone thought or said about it.

As for me, I was always really careful not to spill Kool-Aid on my clothes or even get crumbs on them. Everything had to be just perfect, oh so neat and clean. And I would never chew with my mouth open.

## A Bigger Banquet

God has prepared a banquet table for us, far more enjoyable than even those snack breaks seemed back then.

We see this banquet in the countless gifts of His grace all around us. So how do we handle all these good things He has given us to enjoy?

Like my buddy Buck, do we belly up to the bar and dive in?

Or do we follow the dainty approach? Oftentimes I know I'm only tiptoeing to the table, nibbling around the edges, too worried about my form.

May we all learn to eat and drink of all the grand things God has laid before us. May we have no concern for any Kool-Aid stains on our lips or clothes, or for the crumbs that sprinkle and fall. It will all come out in the wash someday.

So partake from His table without reservation!

# Forgiving and Giving
## *Forgiveness*

Ryan had been upset for over an hour. This was so out of character for him.

Finally Miss Marla asked, "What's going on?"

"I can't find the carved cardinal that Mr. Pfinkston made for me," he explained. Mr. Pfinkston was one of the older patriarchs of the church, and he loved to carve. He had come to Vacation Bible School the day before and handed out carved birds of different kinds. They were prized possessions in the children's hands.

Finally, after settling Ryan down, Miss Marla began to look around the room. She noticed how A. J. had a lump in his back pocket that was strangely shaped like a bird. She approached A. J. and asked him what it was.

A. J. replied sheepishly, "Aw, nothing. Just a rock."

"Well," Miss Marla said, "that must be uncomfortable to sit on; why don't you let me hold it?"

Slowly, he pulled out the carved cardinal, handed it to her, and began to cry.

Ryan was angry when he first saw this. Then he remembered

that A. J. wasn't in attendance yesterday, and he understood why he had taken the cardinal.

Miss Marla told A. J. to give it back to Ryan. Reluctantly, A. J. held out the bird in his hand; Ryan took it. Then, surprisingly, have gave it back. "I forgive you, A. J."

He was not only forgiving ... but *giving*.

A. J. seemed about to cry. "I don't deserve this," he said.

## Complete Forgiveness is a Circle

Forgiveness is the pivot of life with Jesus Christ.

Being born with a sense of justice, especially our own created form of our rights, we naturally avoid forgiveness.

On a larger encompassing level, God our Father is perfect justice. He's the originator of justice, to the point that no one can stand before Him and be self-justified. No one.

For there to be justice, a price must be paid. Jesus Christ, God's Son, paid that price. To anyone who chooses to receive from Him, Jesus gives the justice He purchased by His death on the cross.

We certainly aren't justified by our own merits to stand before a holy and just God. Instead, what we've received is ultimate forgiveness—from the only One whose forgiveness ultimately matters, since all our sin is always against Him.

So what is our response to be, if we've been ultimately forgiven?

It is to *forgive*. Yet if I can't create my own forgiveness, how am I truly to forgive others?

Many times in life I've been betrayed, swindled, and lied to or had my reputation slandered. And I've been abused. I wanted justice. Period. Yet I had no peace. I truly struggled with the command of Jesus Christ to forgive others. Either I could not forgive, or I would not.

Then I realized the depth of my personal sin and the sin of unforgiveness. The first step was realizing my ultimate forgiveness through Jesus Christ. The second revelation was that only He could forgive through me. I didn't have the power in myself; only His power within me could complete this gift of forgiveness. So I asked Him to make me willing to forgive.

I was then able to "pay forward" the gift of forgiveness He'd given me. The result was freedom. I was no longer in bondage to the offenders. And in some cases, even they were set free.

# Gotcha!

## *No You Don't; I Got the Red Flag, Dude!*

It was raining, so for the playtime break, everybody had to stay inside.

Can you imagine seventy-five sugar-charged, runny-nosed kids romping through a pristine church sanctuary?

To somewhat control the chaos, Miss Marla announced a game of hide-and-seek and laid down the rules. Then she gave each person a red flag. *That's a new twist*, everyone thought.

"What's this for?" asked Ryan.

Miss Marla explained, "If you get caught hiding, you have one chance to wave the red flag and get a free pass and not have to go to jail with the other kids."

The odd thing is that everyone quickly forgot about their red flags, since they'd never played by these rules before.

When I was it, I found Ryan and tagged him. He grinned and said, "No big deal, 'cause when I go to jail, I'm just going to get out again!"

"How's that?" I asked.

"'Cause with this red flag, I'll just get out. And when I do, you'll never find me again!"

## Drawn Out

The name *Moses* means "To draw out." God is still drawing His children out of captivity, out of hiding.

Do you feel trapped? Have you ever been imprisoned by unforgiveness, addictions, others' opinions, abuse, fear, or negative feelings? Have you tried everything you and others can think of to break free from these unseen prison bars and chains?

As we read in the Bible about Moses leading the Israelites out of Egypt, we recognize all the miraculous things God did to accomplish this wondrous escape. There were plagues, including the killing of all the firstborn males in every Egyptian household (and remember, Pharaoh was given fair warning about this and could have protected his people). There was also the parting of the Red Sea, as God's people crossed over to safety, after which those same waters closed in to drown all of Pharaoh's army. Then there was God's miraculous provision of food and water for His people in the wilderness. All these things point to the power of God.

God is still in the process of drawing out His people from captivity. Yet the wilderness is not our final destination! Many have accepted His forgiveness yet haven't crossed over into the promised land of freedom. That's what Joshua (whose name means "God saves") accomplished after the Israelites had wondered and wandered in the wilderness for forty years.

Through Jesus, we're not only saved from the penalty of sin, but we're also given power over sin. Through Him alone, working through us by the power of His Holy Spirit, do we have the ability to forgive, to break addictions, to cast off others' opinions, to overcome fear, and to not be ruled by feelings.

# Great Catch!

## *You Can't Play Pitch and Catch with Yourself*

"Okay, everybody outside! Time to play ball!"

You would've thought Miss Marla had hollered, "Fire!" As I ran out the door, I was on my way to my favorite thing in the whole world.

I lived to play softball. But strangely, not everyone was into it like I was. Emily didn't even bring her glove, and she called it a stupid game. Buck reluctantly played with a glove on one hand and a toy John Deere tractor in the other.

Eric, on the other hand, was our Ty Cobb, taking out Keisha at second base in a big play.

Big A. J. was supposed to be the catcher. But at a decisive point late in the game, after the batter hit the ball, A. J. decided he was thirsty, which meant that when I threw the ball to the plate to make the crucial out, no one was there to receive it. A. J. was over by the bench funneling Kool-Aid. The winning run scored, of course, but only Eric and I really cared.

# Intimacy in Giving and Receiving

For a gift to be a gift, it takes a giver *and* receiver. Simple, yet rare.

I've found that most people fall into one of two categories. Many give freely but don't receive freely. Many take freely but don't give freely.

Maturity is found in being open to both. Want to bless someone? Just wash his or her feet. Want to be blessed? Then have your feet washed.

It's easier for me to wash feet than to have my feet washed. I tend to be more of a giver. Giving is normally safer, since it takes less risk—and thus, less intimacy—than receiving. Sometimes my gifts are rejected by others (who thus reject me), but most gifts are at least taken, whether or not they're ever used or appreciated.

But receiving—that's a bigger hazard for me. It means I have to confess or admit I'm needy. That's right; it signifies that I'm lacking in something, needing someone else to provide for me.

Receiving also truly calls for a deeper level of intimacy than giving. That was true for Peter, when Jesus, on His knees, washed Peter's feet. Like Peter, I too must confess my incompleteness and unworthiness. Watching this display of serving on the part of Jesus, Peter and the other disciples received a lesson and a blessing, which they then went forth and shared with the world. For a gift to go forth and multiply, there must be a receiver.

The deepest intimacy comes when we receive the gift of life from Jesus Christ. We then become both receiver and giver.

It takes both to make a gift a gift.

# Say What You Mean, Mean What You Say

## The Truth Comes after the "But…"

"Well, I just told him that I liked him," Bubba was explaining, "but also that he smelled bad and looked funny in those shoes and britches."

Miss Marla was officiating another fight between Bubba and Eric. Eric had arrived as usual in an outfit he put together from the pile of clothes strewn around his room. His mom tried hard to keep his clothes clean and organized, but working two jobs was about all she could accomplish.

Getting Eric dressed and ready for anything was his own job. His father cared more about getting his buzz on and getting Eric out of the house.

Later that day, Miss Marla called Eric's mom and arranged to have some people come over once a week to help her out at home. Miss Marla told her how she'd been in the same position before and that there was no shame in accepting help from other people.

Miss Marla then talked to everyone in our class about love.

She said that love is perfect, that love accepts everyone just as they are, and that love covers over all wrongs.

## Freedom Through Truth

"Faithful are the wounds of a friend, but the kisses of an enemy are deceitful" (Proverbs 27:6 NKJV).

It has taken me years to reconcile truth and love. Beautiful words aren't always truthful, and truthful words aren't always beautiful.

Have you ever noticed when someone starts to tell you something tough, it usually starts with the soft side and then is followed by the "but ..." I've found that the real truth comes after the "but." As in: "I really like being with you, but you make me angry when you (fill in the blank)."

Why do we so often have trouble with the truth, regardless of what it may be? I don't mean in terms of our being positive or negative—those terms are only relative to the truth. Truth is neutral, neither positive nor negative. It's just truth.

Truth can be harmful or hurtful depending on its intention and reception. Causing harm isn't good, but the hurt can be a blessing when its purpose is to break something down that's harming someone. Then that which is broken down can be built back up into something useful.

For so much of my life, I've had the conflict of needing to be liked and wanted, and so I avoided any clashes with people and the potential rejection that might follow. It became very hard for me to be truthful, even when I vaguely realized how the truth would be in everyone's best interest, including my own.

This revealed a deep problem I had with intimacy—for by not risking rejection, I never let anyone see the real me. With me as only an impostor, relationships could never stick since the person these people were dealing with was actually someone else, not the true me.

To compound the problem, I developed a very sharp and quick tongue that made sure I wasn't approachable in matters that dealt with truth. And on occasions when that kind of language on my part wouldn't be socially acceptable, I would use humor to deflect the matter from reaching my soul.

So in dealing with others, I found myself using truth only when I could follow it with a cocoon of flattery.

Freedom, however, is found only in truth: truth about who God is, about who I am, and about the love God has for me.

Jesus told His disciples that by abiding in His word, "you will know the truth, and *the truth will set you free*" (John 8:32). He was telling them the truth about Himself and about the love God the Father was displaying through Him.

In that same chapter of John, Jesus calls Satan the "father of lies" (8:44). Ultimate truth is found in God the Father; anything else is a lie, regardless of how nice or right or fair it may sound.

It wasn't until I deeply realized God's love for me that I could bear to live in truth. The light of the truth was so bright that it left me nowhere to hide. I couldn't hide from the fact of His love, or from the fact that in my own flesh, nothing good dwells. Truly the only good in me is Jesus Christ dwelling there and overpowering my sinful nature, so that I might live now in the freedom that results from His presence.

I'm slowly learning about the helpfulness of the truth. If it can ultimately be used by the other person to lead to freedom, then sharing the truth can be helpful. Thankfully, I now have friends in my life who will tell me the truth because they love me and want to see me grow more into the likeness of Jesus Christ.

The next time you're looking for the truth, listen closely to what people say after the "but." And for yourself, consider taking the "but" out of your conversations—simply speak the truth in love, for only love is the truth.

# WWMMD? (What Would Miss Marla Do?)

## *Close, but Wrong Question*

Keisha, A. J., and Bubba had a dilemma. There were two cookies, three mouths, and six hands.

Keisha was the smallest but also the quickest. Yet A. J. arrived first to the plate. And Bubba—well, he was the biggest.

The argument started with A. J.'s insistence that he was there first. But Keisha grabbed a cookie and protested, "I haven't had *any*, and y'all have had three!"

Bubba then shouted, "What are you babies gonna do about it, anyway? 'Cause I will body-slam you! Is it worth gettin' a whuppin'?"

Emily saw their squabble and said, "What would Miss Marla do?"

This at least stopped them in their tracks for a moment, until Keisha piped up and said, "I know she would want me to have this cookie, since I haven't had any."

"No," A. J. disagreed. "She would say, 'First come, first served!'"

Bubba, true to form, exclaimed, "She would say that I'm the biggest, and it takes more to feed a bigger cow!"

Then Ryan stepped closer and pointed to Miss Marla standing across the room. "Why don't we just ask her?"

## Not WWJD, but AJWTD (Ask Jesus What to Do)

The book written by Charles Sheldon in 1896, *In His Steps*, has long been popularized in our American Christian culture with its signature question, "What Would Jesus Do?" But such a question can easily remove from us the power we have in the ability to ask Jesus Himself, "What are we to do?"

When we try answering the question of what Jesus would do, we have a great ability to rationalize our desires, to cast the net of "sounds good to me" and then validate our preferences with "this feels right."

To fully ask, "What would Jesus do?" and get an answer that's at least close to being right, you would have to know Jesus very well. This means studying His life, including His conversations with the crowds and with His disciples. Even then, you would have to guess on an answer for your own situation, an answer that would be filtered through your own "good" intentions.

Going deeper into His Word, we might get closer to a correct answer. We could try consulting the best biblical scholars, yet I think that if we asked ten of them what Jesus would do in a given contemporary situation, we very well could get ten different answers.

I suggest a better approach. The right question needs to be asked of the right person: *Jesus, what would You have me do?*

As believers, our very life now is "hidden with Christ in God" (Colossians 3:3). This seals our destination: *heaven*. However, many have stopped here with their understanding of this truth and have abandoned His power at this point, trying to figure out their lives without His power and input.

The Bible reminds us that Jesus is *in* us (Romans 8:10; 2 Corinthians 13:5). With Jesus Christ alive and living in us through His Holy Spirit, we can fulfill the destiny He has designed for us, knowing that He'll lead us to accomplish His purpose.

In the Great Commission Jesus gave us, He closed with these words: "Surely *I am with you always*, to the very end of the age" (Matthew 28:20). So we have Him 100 percent *with* us as well as *in* us, and we are in Him. Therefore, in every situation where we need guidance on what to do, we can go directly to *Him* and ask *Him* for that guidance. With the Holy Spirit leading us through His Word, we can know that He'll answer the questions we ask.

Then we experience this reality: "It is God who works in you to will and to act in order to fulfill his good purpose" (Philippians 2:13). In some other versions, that last phrase is translated as "for His good pleasure." So there we have it: *His* work, *His* will and action, *His* good purpose and pleasure.

We're never alone, and we're never without perfect direction from our perfect Lord and Savior, Jesus Christ.

So ask the right Person the right question.

# Grace Isn't Just a Word
## *Grace Applied*

"Gather around, children," Miss Marla said. "It's time for a story."

Buck loved stories. When Miss Marla embarked on her narrative about a wee little man called Zacchaeus, you could see that Buck (being a big kid) already felt sorry for this guy. But his look changed to a frown when she told how Zacchaeus made himself rich by taking money from those who had little or nothing to begin with.

Then she said Zacchaeus had to climb a tree to see Jesus—another interesting detail, since Buck liked tree-climbing. When Jesus looked up and saw him, he told Zacchaeus to come on down so he could eat with him. Zacchaeus was so happy, he hurried down and told everyone he was giving half his money to the poor. He would even repay four times as much money to anybody he'd stolen from.

*Now why would anybody do that?* You could see that question in Buck's eyes.

# The Fruit of Repentance

Jesus explained it this way: Zacchaeus had been lost; now he was found and saved.

So did Zacchaeus get there simply by paying back all that money?

No, Zacchaeus didn't buy this grace; this grace bought him. He was simply applying the grace he'd received. He was living it out in what the Bible calls bearing "fruit in keeping with repentance" (Matthew 3:8).

Are you stuck—unable to say yes to the salvation God offers you through His Son Jesus Christ because you don't think you can live the life He'll call you to live? Or having accepted His salvation, are you stuck in being unable to live out the new life He has given you? Do you feel mired in the self-serving purpose of being a better person because this is what you think salvation is all about? Are you convicted by the internal evidence of not measuring up to what you think you should be as a Christian?

There is grace—and there's grace *applied*.

God, in His mercy, through our acceptance of Jesus Christ, forgives us of all our sins. When did He die for you? It was before you committed your first sin. And it covers all the way to your last sin.

His grace means He gives us what we don't deserve. That's the unconditional love of God through His Son Jesus Christ. And this grace isn't a static, one-time thing. It's an eternal, ongoing experience of the love of God through Jesus Christ. This grace keeps giving, every nanosecond of our lives.

We apply this gift of grace as we move forward—out of

ourselves, and into the life of this world around us where He calls us to enter. His grace *through* us offers hope to that dying world.

We can't continue to live in spiritual power if we're living only out of gratefulness for what God has done in saving us. That motivation will soon wear off in the everyday grind of life. No, we're empowered by the Holy Spirit living in us to *keep living out this grace*.

To bear the fruit of repentance, we must be continually connected to the vine; from the vine comes the sap to produce the fruit. We're grateful for the vine, yes; but gratefulness doesn't produce fruit. The sap from the vine through the branches produces the fruit.

God's grace saves you. Now allow that same grace to empower you to bear fruit in keeping with repentance.

# Live with the End in Sight
## *It's Really Just the Beginning*

"Come on, Bubba, hit the ball!" Eric hollered.

It was a close softball game, but all the money was ridin' on big Bubba. When he connected, he could hit the ball a mile. Yet actually hitting it was the challenge. Nobody could swing with such uncontrolled abandonment as Bubba.

Up to bat again, Bubba threw his big body at the first two pitches and fell down each time.

Determined, Eric shouted at his teammate again: "There are girls on that other team, and we'll never hear the end of this if we lose!"

Timothy the Frogboy croaked out more encouragement: "The winners get barbecued ribs!"

That was just the motivation Bubba needed. This time he patiently waited for the pitch, then lunged with all his might.

And he finally connected. The ball sailed out over the ditch into the schoolyard across the street. Emily, the fastest kid on the other team, took off for the ball like a hungry hound chasing a rabbit.

Now ol' Bubba was as slow as he was big. It looked like he was taking a victory grand-slam trot. Meanwhile Emily had retrieved the ball and hustled back toward us. She leaned back to make a desperate toss to Natasha at the plate.

After slowly rounding third base, Bubba stepped on a red Frisbee lying on the baseline and slipped. Digging and clawing, he eventually lumbered home in time to miss the tag by Natasha—who was really just taking a swipe, as she ran the other way to avoid any broken bones from a collision with Bubba.

Victory! And defeat.

## Living for True Victory

Several thoughts about life come to mind here. It's not if you win or lose but how you play the game. Are you even *in* the game? What's the game of life you're playing? What does victory in your game of life look like?

I've read many books and heard many talks and sermons that encouraged us to imagine our own funeral. You know the scenario. What will people there be thinking and saying about you? Will anybody cry? If they sing a song that represents your life, will it be "I Did It My Way"? Or "I'd Rather See a Sermon than Hear One Any Day"? What unchangeable truths about your life will be revealed on that day? Did your life have meaning? Did all those things you worried about really make any difference?

But as a recovering people-pleaser, I want to put a twist on this discussion.

You are unique; God says you are fearfully and wonderfully made. I encourage you not to live your life in light of what others will think and say of you at your funeral, since they're neither the judge nor the jury.

We have a Maker who has designed us to be *His* possession and to live out our lives to *His* pleasure, not to our own or to another's pleasure. Through our surrender to Him, we allow Him to give us the life to live. We can have the full knowledge of trusting Him—all the while knowing, as we've seen, that He's always at work within us "to will and to act in order to fulfill his good purpose" (Philippians 2:13). And He alone is the One before whom all will stand when they die.

For unbelievers standing naked before Him, He'll render judgment based on His righteous perfection—and they'll fall short.

For believers—those who trust in Christ, who rely and wholly lean on Christ for what He has done for them through His life, death, and resurrection—there will be judgment and reward for their true works that He led them to do, empowered and inspired by Christ Himself.

So I encourage you to consider not what others will think or say when you die. Instead, look past all that into eternity—and choose life, not death. Then the life you live here will have meaning greater than yourself, for it will be a life uniquely lived, fulfilling the Father's true desire for *you*, His child.

Prepare for that coming day by keeping these truths in mind:

"And do not grieve the Holy Spirit of God, with whom you were sealed for the day of redemption" (Ephesians 4:30).

"For we know that our old self was crucified with him so that the body ruled by sin might be done away with, that we should no longer be slaves to sin" (Romans 6:6).

# Judging
## *Intentions vs. Actions*

"My daddy taught me better," said Timmy. "I would never do something like that to you!"

"I didn't think you would really fall," Bubba replied. "It was just sorta kinda like a trip. But you were funny-looking, dancing around and trying not to fall and spilling your Kool-Aid all over Emily. It looked like something out of a movie."

A. J. had seen it. "Yeah," he said, "I wouldn't ever do that to anyone either, 'cause they might hurt themselves." Meanwhile he took two cookies from Ryan's plate when he wasn't looking, since all the other cookies were gone.

"Yeah, Bubba," Eric said, "that was an awful way to treat Timmy. I hate people who pick on other people." He was saying this just after talking about how stupid Bubba looked in his cowboy boots and short britches.

Keisha chimed in. "I think all of you are mean—the way you say one thing and do another. I heard some of you making fun of my cornrowed hair and my tan. I ain't never talked about y'all that way." Of course Keisha had a habit of making fun of others who couldn't run as fast as she could, or add numbers in their head the way she could.

At the end of the day, everyone had found some comment to make about something bad that others did, but that they of course would never do. Yet instead of feeling good about themselves, each one went home feeling something was wrong.

Was something wrong with them … or with everyone else?

*Yes.*

Dude, there's a big log in your eye!

## A Life of Forgiveness, not Judging

Have you ever noticed how the really bad sins are always those that *other* people have?

Here's something I've often observed: someone who doesn't drink alcohol is gossiping about the awfulness of someone who's struggling with alcoholism, trying to be rid of this demon he or she wrestles with.

Have you noticed that church people don't gossip, they "share"? We seem to have a deep propensity to focus on others as a need to measure up just a little taller.

The deep truth is that we all fall short of the glory of God. "If we claim to be without sin, we deceive ourselves and the truth is not in us" (1 John 1:8).

Jesus Christ didn't come to make us better people; He came to redeem us from our sins and give us *His* life to be lived through us, for He took all our past, current, and future sins upon Himself when He died upon the cross.

"Why do you look at the speck of sawdust in your brother's

eye and pay no attention to the plank in your own eye?" (Luke 6:41). We're forgiven, and we live a life of forgiveness to be poured out on everyone we meet, regardless of the sins they commit against us.

Jesus is more than the great equalizer of men; He is a *Redeemer* who sets us right before our just God. We no longer have to measure up to anyone; nor does anyone need to measure up to us. We're free to live a life of non-comparison.

Our shortcomings are seen by God only through the life of His perfect Son, Jesus. So as we have been forgiven, we forgive—and we can throw the unbalance of our own judgment in the sea of His forgiveness.

# Sliding Down the Banister of Life

## *Sometimes We Just Need a Push*

"Come on, Earl, you can do it!" said Ryan.

"No he can't," said one bully down below. "He's afraid of everything, even worms."

"Leave him alone," Emily pleaded.

The scene was playtime on the slides out on the church playground. It was obvious that time stood still for Earl, as he quivered at the top of the high slide and looked around dazed. He knew he was afraid of heights, but enough of the boys had shamed him that he decided he would show them up.

Now, much to his shame, he was stuck. His fear had paralyzed him.

Finally, above the shouts of taunting, Earl heard a still, small voice. It was Ryan, on the steps behind him. Ryan, too, was afraid of heights, but he'd climbed up anyway behind Earl.

"Earl," he whispered, "you can do it!"

The next thing we saw was Earl and Ryan sliding toward the bottom. They hit the ground, tumbling like rags wrapped around a bouncy ball. Yet they emerged from their entanglement with shouts of victory—their own and those of everyone around them.

It never would have happened without encouragement.

## Encouragement Creates Momentum

To *encourage* means to inspire with courage, spirit, or confidence.

I love the famous words from the Bible that carry this inspiration: "Be strong and courageous. Do not be afraid; do not be discouraged" (Joshua 1:9).

God knows we're not courageous people. Each one of us has something we fear.

It is said that people's most common fear is that of public speaking. There are countless other human fears that have been identified, even the fear of clowns, of bubbles, or of bellybuttons.

But what we really fear most is *life*. We often live small—not taking risks for fear that things won't turn out like we want. It's just another way of us trying to be God.

Earl and Ryan had a fear of falling from up high, or at least the fear of the sudden stop when hitting the ground. We're all afraid our lives will meet tragedy, unless we live "safe."

I'm convinced that we cannot truly live without courage. I also believe God will often use others to encourage us.

"Encourage one another daily," the Bible commands us, "as long as it is called 'Today,' so that none of you may be hardened by sin's deceitfulness" (Hebrews 3:13). We're to encourage daily because we *all* need it. We need it, and we need to give it.

We need it because sin's deceitfulness is constantly telling us that surely God isn't with us or for us; we're constantly hearing the whispered words of doom. But the blessing of God is that He encourages us to do things we cannot do on our own, to prove that only He can do them through us—thus glorifying *Him*, and not us.

Even our encouragement of others by His Spirit shows the wonder of our need to be a part of His body.

So make a choice today to both give and receive encouragement—thus creating the momentum to live your life to the fullness that only God can accomplish through you.

# Stand or Fall
## Short of the Truth

Bubba pushed Emily (who was half his size) out of his way when she cut in line for the chocolate cookies. He quickly justified his action: "My daddy said to stand up for myself when somebody does me wrong!"

The fact is, Emily had been near the front of the line earlier, but seeing Ryan drop his ball cap, she had stepped over to pick it up for him.

"Too bad for you, girl," Bubba said.

Emily started to cry—not so much from losing her place in the refreshments line but because she felt she was being persecuted for doing something right.

Ryan realized what was happening. He stepped up to Bubba and told him to apologize to Emily. To do this was a fearless act for Ryan, since Bubba, ever the bully, stood a full head taller.

Bubba responded, "I ain't backing off, 'cause I gotta stand up for the rules. My daddy said if you don't stand for something, you'll fall for anything."

Ryan and Emily gave up and shuffled to the end of the line.

# The Worlds Views vs. Gods Views

I've collected old sayings since I was a teenager. I often found wisdom in them and have been intrigued by how they're passed from generation to generation. There was a time when I didn't question them; I just admired some nugget of knowledge to be found within each one.

Then several years ago, I found myself being convicted while quoting this one Bubba liked about our falling for anything if we don't stand for something. I realized that a more accurate statement would be this: "If you don't stand for the *truth*, you've already fallen."

I wonder how many times I've stood up for my need to be right, look good, protect my reputation, etc., only to have fallen short of the truth.

How paradoxical is the gospel of Jesus Christ, from the heart of God: *The first shall be last; in surrendering we're set free; by losing our lives we gain them; in dying with Him we're reborn.*

Just like building a house on a firm foundation, we must start from a position of truth to stand and not fall.

So question first whether you're standing upon truth and falling for love—or whether you're standing for being "right" while actually falling for a lie.

# What If

## What If What?

"What if the cookies are all gone? What if they run out of Kool-Aid? What if my dad forgets to come and get me, and I miss my baseball game?"

These rapid-fire questions came from Eric. He was always worried about something. Because of his insecure home life, uncertainty had become his closest companion.

Ryan, always a comforter, tried to calm Eric. "Don't worry," he said. But this did little good because Eric was slow to trust anyone or anything.

Ryan kept trying. He assured Eric that there were always reserves of cookies and Kool-Aid. "And my mom can always give you a ride to your game if you need it."

Eric listened. "Yeah, maybe," he said. But he was still doubtful. He wanted what he wanted, and he was afraid he wouldn't get it.

Ryan stepped in again, this time drawing on his own experience. "You know, sometimes things don't always turn out the way I think they should. But it seems like my mom always makes things right in the end."

# The Root of Worry

What if things just haven't turned out the way you think they should? Aren't you right to worry?

*Worry.* Has it become your closest companion? Have you ever wondered why some people just have a tendency to worry more than others? Are some just wired that way?

I think it helps to look at the root of worry: *I want to be the center of my life.* I was born that way. It's part of original sin. I desire to be in control of everything, from input to output, and all the results. I'm hardwired to trust in myself. That's the root. It reflects my reluctance to trust God for everything, from taking care of myself to things turning out the way I think they should. It's setting myself on the throne of my life and world and telling God how I think everything should operate.

Sin is seeking to get my needs met outside of Jesus Christ.

If I believe He is King, then I can trust He'll work through me to provide for my needs. I can trust that the resulting outcomes will bring glory to Him through my life.

Our responsibility is always to *respond to Him.* My response is to do what He leads me to do, to trust Him for the power to do it, and to embrace the ultimate results, whether or not they please my expectations.

My prayer is that you no longer live in the land of "what if."

Don't live in the past by always thinking, *If I had only …*

Don't live in the present land of *What if God doesn't come through this time?*

And don't live in the future land of *What if things don't turn out like I think they should?* That's a land inhabited by guaranteed unfulfillment and death.

May you live instead in the fulfillment of trusting God for everything. He's redeeming the past, providing for the now, and completing your destiny of glorifying and enjoying Him forever.

May you recognize the truth that you *can't* … but He *can* and *will*.

# Singin in the Key of Free
## *When Did I Stop Skipping?*

Timmy couldn't dance, and Timmy couldn't sing.

"Okay, children," Miss Marla would gladly announce, "now we get to sing!" It wasn't enough that we were to sing along with whatever she was leading; we also had to hold hands, kick our legs, wave our arms, and hoky-poky all together.

It was bittersweet for me, since I had Timmy the Frogboy on one side of me but angelic Emily on the other. Timmy would squeal and squeak like a bad Kung Fu martial artist. I couldn't hear Emily's voice, but her smile made up the difference.

This had to be Timmy's best part of the day, for he would exert all his energy, like trying to pull a bottle down through the Coke machine slot without paying. He was joyously oblivious to everyone around him; it really didn't matter what he sounded or looked like, for he was living large! To say it was a joyful noise doesn't suffice; horrible sound and sight capture the moment much better.

When we finished all the racket and the gyrating, Timmy looked satisfied, like someone having finished a well-eaten dinner. I asked him one day, "What's the deal with you and this hoky-poky commotion?"

"I really like it!" he said. It was that simple.

Unlike Timmy, some of the other kids could sing, some could dance, and some could even do both. Yet through the years, it amazes me how many cease to do either.

## A Child Again

When did we stop singing and dancing? When did we outgrow skipping? Did we discover that others' opinions of our "talents" snuffed out the songs and dances of our life? Did we just get overburdened by everything we've stuffed in our bags? Have the floors we walk on become slippery from all our spilled lives? Have we become hoarse from all our screaming demands to have our own way? Have we become crippled by the blows of betrayal when we try to live as God designed?

I pray that God reveals His love to you. May it cause you to become as a little child again, knowing how deeply He loves you and how He dances wildly over you as you come into His presence.

May you start skipping again in His presence as you embrace the joy He has for you and your life.

# Who is That?

## *Foreigner, Brother, Sister*

"Ryan," Buck asked, "who's that dude that came with you and Miss Marla?" The visitor was a man never seen before by the rest of us.

"Oh, that's Abdul," Ryan answered. "He's staying with us this week. He's a missionary."

"Is he one of those Arabs I saw on the news?" Bubba asked.

"No," Ryan replied. "He's from Afghanistan. He helps children in his country by bringing them food and sharing about the love Jesus has for them. That's what my mom said."

"Then why's he here with us?" Eric asked. "Don't those children over there still need him?"

"Well, I guess they do," Ryan acknowledged. "Last night, he shared with us how the children don't have enough to eat. He also said some people hate him because he's following Jesus. He said that his wife's family even tried to kill him because of that."

"Why would someone want to kill him," A. J. asked, "if he loves children like Jesus does?"

"He said that in his country, the most important thing isn't people, but it's having power and forcing everyone to submit to their religion. He said some people there think that children aren't as important as doing what they tell you to do."

Later, during our story time, Abdul told us all about himself.

# Total Dependence

"Abdul" is a real person. Not long ago I heard him speak to our church and to a small group about his life and the amazing things God has done to him and through him.

It was amazing to hear how he was once in training to become a martyr for Islam, but through his reading of the Bible and the conviction of his heart, he believed in the love of God through His Son Jesus Christ.

He told how he had lost his wife and three sons because of his choice. He spoke of how his family and his wife's family refused to be with him, and they had threatened his life. But he said that the love of God in his heart for the suffering in his country compelled him to give God's love by helping orphans and others affected by his country's thirty years of war. He said that because of God's love, he still loves his family and those who have tried to kill him, even his enemies.

He said it might appear that he has lost everything, but actually he has gained that which can never be taken away—the love of God through Jesus Christ His Son. He said this life is only a vapor; compared to living eternally with God, our lives here are very short.

As Jim Elliot said, "He is no fool who gives what he cannot keep to gain that which he cannot lose."

As I listened to Abdul, I was reminded of these words of Jesus:

"I have told you these things, so that in me you may have peace. In this world you will have trouble. But take heart! I have overcome the world" (John 16:33).

I've realized just how different my walk with Jesus is than the life experienced by most of my brothers and sisters around the world, especially in countries that are hostile to Christianity. The challenges I face pale in comparison to the costs they know. I may lose a possible friend or business deal because of my stand for Christ, but there's no real risk of losing my life.

I was convicted by the things that I worry about, things that have nothing to do with advancing the love of Jesus Christ to a world in desperate need for the hope we have in Him.

I question why God placed Abdul in such dangerous conditions, while I live in the luxury of safety.

Abdul spoke also about how dependent he is upon Jesus to supply his every need—from the funds and the food to take care of children, to his own personal safety.

I realized then how blessed he was to be living in such total dependence upon the One who keeps him. I saw how dependent I'd become on myself and on the resources God had given me, instead of truly relying on God as my all-sufficiency. I realized I'd been assessing my life from a secular worldview, not from God's view.

The ultimate reality is that God is our Creator and the One who loves us. He delights in His children, regardless of where He has placed us or the conditions in which we find ourselves.

We can know there's blessing in every trial and tribulation, because those situations lead us toward resting in His loving safety.

There's much more to life than the time we spend here in this world. The only true living we can experience is through the life Jesus Christ has given us and now lives through us here on earth. And when we give up our grasp on everything we hold dear in this life, He gives us new life that will never be separated from Him, both here on earth and in heaven with Him forever.

He is our treasure that never depletes.

# A Day in the Life of a Coke Bottle

## The Great Exchange

"Ryan, where did you get all that money?" Buck asked.

Ryan had pulled the change from his pocket to show everyone. It amounted to more than three dollars' worth. He then proceeded to tell everyone the story behind his newfound fortune.

"I've been going around the neighborhood collecting empty pop bottles and taking them down to Tapp's grocery and getting money in return. I take my wagon around picking up discarded bottles and even asking my neighbors if they have any extras. I take them back to my house and clean them up real good and then go to the store and trade 'em for nickels.

"I've learned a lot in my new business. Last week on my way to the store with a full wagon, I found two old bottles full of mud, and I put 'em in my wagon. When I got to the grocery store, I asked Mr. Tapp if I could use his garden hose around back to clean those two I'd just found, so I could get a couple more nickels. He told me, 'It doesn't matter if they're clean or not, 'cause the bottling company will clean and purify them before they get filled up again with pop.' So it doesn't matter if they're clean or not—they're all worth the same!"

*Whether clean or not ... all worth the same.* Out of the mouths of babes!

## Redeemed and Restored

I still remember having the thought that I must first clean up my act before Jesus would accept someone like me.

To those around me, it looked like I already had my life together. I looked like a real clean Coke bottle. But I'd been cleaning myself up with only the window dressing of good works and words. On the inside, the bacteria of sin was eating away, rendering me useless for fulfilling God's original purposes.

But in Jesus, we all get cleaned up through His washing alone. In Jesus, we're all worth the same.

# Who Are You?
## *Whose Are You?*

"I'm Superman!" exclaimed A. J.

"Well, I'm gonna be Thor," said Buck.

"I'm Flash, 'cause I'm fast," said Eric.

"I'm Batman today," said Timmy.

Ryan sighed. "Well, I guess I have to be Robin again."

"If *I* had to be Robin," Buck told him, "I wouldn't play!"

And so the daily game of superheroes began. Each kid was trumping the other with their own special powers, like rock, paper, and scissors. No one won, but hard play and fantasy ruled the day.

When it was all said and done, the question was asked, "Who's the greatest superhero?"

Ryan, always so quick to see beyond the others, declared, "I think Jesus could whip them all!"

## Your Hero Says a Lot about Who You Are

Remember those days? We played fantasy games that truly reflected the condition of our hearts and desires. The girls were princesses needing a prince. The boys were princes looking for dragons to slay and princesses to rescue. Our deep and true need to be heroes was being played out without inhibition.

We didn't see ourselves as kings, because we knew that was our dad's role. Even those kids without dads knew that deep down inside they needed one.

I truly believe God has put eternity in our hearts, just as He said. Each of us knows that there's *something more*. We long to be with Someone who perfectly loves us in a place where things are the way they really should be.

Yet for most, we continue to be our own heroes and end up being victims to the lie that we can save ourselves. Those who haven't accepted the offer from Jesus Christ of salvation and new life will continue to play out the role of being their own heroes or victims—and will fail to gain the kingdom God desires for them. They remain orphans scrapping for their next crumb, reaching the end of the fantasy without rescue.

Nearly as tragic are those who have been rescued by the Hero, yet continue to live as if they're orphans. They play out their fantasy of rescuing themselves and others, living off of scraps from under the banquet table of the King.

We must embrace our identity as children of the almighty King. We're seated in heavenly places with Jesus, our Hero, that He might supply all our needs according to His riches in glory.

This is no fantasy; this is reality. Our identity is that of a prince or princess living now in His kingdom under His rule. Our deepest longing for a hero is realized when we surrender to our identity in Jesus Christ as sons and daughters of a King who rescues us and leads us out of captivity into a life of victory that has already been won.

It's a victory not just for ourselves but for all the orphans who are scrapping for their next piece of daily bread. To them we give freely the bread of life—which only increases our desire to one day sit at the banquet table of God, our heavenly Daddy.

# The Stress of Uncertainty
## *Finding the Unchanging*

It was a day to remember to be forgotten!

"Where are the chocolate cookies?" asked Bubba. "I want chocolate ones, not these!"

"Yeah, and this Kool-Aid tastes like water," complained Eric.

A groundswell of rebellion seemed to be rising from the kids. They were arguing about how everything was different today. There seemed to be no organization, and the kids were starting to dart around like protons, headed in any and every direction, both physically and emotionally.

Small fights broke out among the boys. The girls were incessantly belittling each other. Even the daily volunteers were at their wits' end, not knowing what to do.

Finally, Emily asked, "Where's Miss Marla?"

Miss Cathy frowned as she said, "Ryan is sick today, so Miss Marla stayed home to take care of him."

Emily looked confused. Then she uttered the question on many minds: "What's going to happen to us?"

# Sheep Need a Shepherd

Have you ever noticed how much people need certainty?

I'm amazed by how I spent most of my life, from childhood to adulthood, trying to order my world, inside and out. It seemed as though I always lived under the expectation of some impending doom. There was always a feeling that both my inner and outer worlds were out of control.

No matter how hard I tried to be optimistic, my rose-colored glasses kept slipping down my nose, revealing this world as it truly is—a dangerous place in which to live. Everything from my fear of rejection to my fear of success left me dying daily inside, trying to grab for life through all the wrong measures. From overachieving to hiding my sins, I dragged through the days trying to find security.

Finally, worn out from pretending that both the world and I were okay, I surrendered my life to the One who created me and designed me to live in union with Him. I found a peace in the security of knowing that He is God and I am not. It sounds trite, yet it's the only answer I've found that allows me to truly live in freedom—the freedom of knowing I'm forgiven and knowing He's leading me daily to live in the ultimate security of His love.

For about five years after I accepted Christ as my Savior, I continued to want to be lord of my own life, a life that later I realized was actually no longer mine, but His. Through His not-so-gentle conviction of my I-can-take-it-from-here attitude, God showed me that He was more than able to take care of me. He would meet not only my inner and outward needs, but also my need for the ability to live out this life He'd purchased for me, a life spent in loving the people He wanted to love through me.

I needed to realize that in this life and world, there really is Someone who will never change. "Every good and perfect gift is from above, coming down from the Father of the heavenly lights, *who does not change* like shifting shadows" (James 1:17). This verse assures me that there's no changing in God Himself. He's the one consistent, almighty, never-changing being in charge of all things.

I've memorized several verses that lead me to this assurance, including this one: "And we know that in all things God works for the good of those who love him, who have been called according to his purpose" (Romans 8:28). I've found that this word *all* really does mean all! Regardless of the injustice, pain, trials, or tribulations we experience, He'll work all things together for our good and His purpose.

He's truly my security eternally! And eternity, by the way, includes my yesterdays, my today, and my tomorrows.

# What Kind of Soil?

## *Amazing What Can Grow Through the Cracks*

The plastic cups were already showing signs of life as the seeds we planted started to grow and sprout some type of bud. It had only been a week, but those grow-lights Miss Marla had brought from home were magically working.

Funny, though, how some cups had lots of growth while others looked like nothing was going to grow at all.

As we were playing outside, where we'd each dug out some dirt to put in our cups, we saw the very same plants sprouting. Some were being trampled where we were playing, and others were sprouting heartily through cracks in the sidewalk alongside where we'd dug some of the dirt.

So some plants were growing in the cups and some were not. Some were growing beside the sidewalk, and some were growing through the cracks of the sidewalk.

# The Way of Growth

It's amazing how life has a way of growing in different places. Let us first consider that the seed is perfect. The seed is representative of the faith that God sows into our lives. The soil represents us. The result of growth depends upon the soil, not the seed or where the soil may be located. Even in different and unusual places we can still see growth.

Like the story above, we can find growth beside the sidewalk or even through the cracks of the sidewalk. It isn't about where the soil is located, but the condition of the soil that makes the difference. Yet, in some cases we don't find the sprouted seed in the cups where we would most expect it. This sounds a lot like my yard a month after I sow it. The seemingly most perfect places for the grass seed to root and sprout doesn't always have grass, yet the cracked sidewalk sometimes does!

Was there different seed sown in some places? No. The difference is the soil. I realize that the saying, "Bloom where you are planted," is often overused. However, it does reveal that the location of our seed isn't the crucial factor.

The key is that the seed blooms and grows.

I've often heard people say, "If only I lived in another neighborhood I wouldn't have these problems." "If only I could work at this place I could do more good." "If I had a different spouse or different friends I could love more effectively." Of course, there are exceptions in some cases, but usually we allow these to be excuses that keep us from allowing our roots to grow deep in the soil. We allow these excuses to prevent God's love from blooming right where He has planted us.

Ask yourself, "How am I limiting the seed that God has

planted in me to grow?" How can we expect to love others who are blooming somewhere else if we are not loving those who are planted right beside us?

Regardless of where you are now planted in your life, the choice is always yours to bloom and grow. Perfect seed can grow wherever it is planted and thrive in the most unlikely of conditions.

# The Battle
## *Oh, Behave!*

"Stay out of this!" Bubba shouted to the boys gathering around him. "Or I'll give you some of this too!" He was pelting Eric on the ground.

Once the fight started, kids came running toward it—some out of curiosity, some out of pity, and some to help.

"What did Eric do?" A. J. asked.

"They started talking about each of their daddies," Buck explained, "and it escalated to a whuppin' when Bubba called Eric's daddy a drunk, and then Eric said at least his daddy wasn't a stupid ol' plowboy like Bubba's."

Ryan ran and got Miss Marla to come and help, because everyone else was just watching and doing nothing.

When Miss Marla arrived on the scene, she separated the boys and gave them some time to cool down.

Then she told them, "This is not who we are. We are the children of a loving God. He sent Jesus, His own Son, to show that He loves us and that we no longer have to live as though we're orphans without dads. Jesus loves us and gives us His love so we'll accept and love one another—even love those who don't love us. Only Jesus living in us can make that happen.

"I pray that each one of you children here will come to know and really experience that you're His children."

## What Happened That Terrible Yet Great Day?

The shed blood of Jesus Christ covers our sins. It covers those wrong things we've done in the past, as well as the wrong things we'll do while continuing to live in this body.

His death deals the final blow to who we *were*—that old person who existed before He gave us new life. The recognition of this truth is something I call 2:20 Vision, from Galatians 2:20. Paul's words in that verse speak to the fact that our old self was crucified with Christ on the cross. The death He died, He died for us. The life we now live is the one He lives in us.

So we now have a new life. Paul also says in 2 Corinthians 5:17 that whoever is *in* Christ is a new creation; the old has gone away and the new has arrived. That's *real life*—true life that never is to die, that is never to be separated from Him.

So we've become *saints* (that's who we *are,* our true identity), yet in this life we still sin. We're no longer just *sinners* (that's who we *were*, our old identity); we're sinners now saved by grace. And that word *saved* is past tense—accomplished once and for all by what Jesus did for us.

So we have a new identity. The life we now live, we live by faith in the One who saved us and keeps us, Jesus Christ. We're no longer our old selves ("the old man," Ephesians 4:22 NKJV), trying to be good on our own power, but new people ("the new man,"

4:24), trusting in the power of the life of Jesus Christ through His Holy Spirit to keep us and lead us in living a truly holy life. Our part is not to try to do better, because we can't really do that in our own power; our part is to surrender to the power of God living out *His* life through us. We're to live out our inheritance *now*—rather than thinking of our inheritance as only in the future.

We're *already* living in eternity, not just waiting to live with Him in heaven. Heaven will be the place where we no longer need His power within us to conquer the sin that resides in our earthly bodies. We'll have new, glorious bodies, and we'll live in the total presence of our heavenly Father, doing only His will—for there will no longer be any sin within us, or the opposition that always arises from that.

Knowing our true identity in Christ allows us to live in the freedom He has already claimed for us, and in His power at work within us. His blood removes the penalty of sin; His life frees us from the power of sin.

Recognize who you already are in Christ, and experience the power of Christ in you to live out the newness of His own life within you. This is the freedom He has given you to fulfill the destiny He has called you to. Give up continuing to try in your own power to live out His calling. Surrender—and let His power work through you for His glory, not yours.

"We have this treasure in jars of clay to show that this all-surpassing power is from God and not from us" (2 Corinthians 4:7).

# How High?

## *Measuring Our Dreams*

Zach was a good bit shorter than everyone else his age. Everyone noticed, and of course, some commented.

"Stand up, Zach," Bubba shouted when Zach went to the front of the room to explain his Lew Alcindor poster. The poster was life-sized and about three times taller than Zach. It took Miss Marla and two teachers with long poles to hold up the poster while Zach talked.

Zach explained that Lew Alcindor was his hero because he was so tall. He said he dreamed of being tall like him some day, so he could buy his mom everything she needed, including food. He said he would also buy clothes and toys for his seven brothers and sisters.

Zach had a dream. His dream was bigger than himself, yet it was about taking care of those he loved. It was not for Zach's glory but for the glory of giving to those who took care of him and who had so little except love to give him.

# From Me to Thee

When a man in a boat throws his anchor toward shore and then pulls on the rope, he often gets the sense that he's pulling the land toward himself.

It's "natural" for us to think we're the center of everything, even when all nature shows us otherwise. Each of us can feel totally alone in our thoughts even when surrounded by thousands of people. In certain tough moments, it's easy to think *we're the only one*—unaware that this exact thought occurs at times to everyone!

You think you're different and unique; well, you are—and yet, you're not. You share the same common humanity, the same nature as everyone ever born. Yet there's no one exactly like you.

You're unique, for example, in that your dreams are your own. What do you dream about? Fortune or fame? Enhancing the lives of those around you?

As I reflect on my life, I can see the progression from *me* to *Thee*. Only in the last several years have I surrendered my dreams to God. God has continued to place people in my life who've helped me in this, allowing me to evaluate my dreams and to see that this life really isn't about me getting all I want. It's about Christ living His life through me, letting me live out my dream (and His purpose) of making a difference here and now for all eternity.

It's a life I can pursue in peace, free from anxiety: "Do not be anxious about anything, but in every situation, by prayer and petition, with thanksgiving, present your requests to God. *And the peace of God*, which transcends all understanding, will guard your hearts and your minds in Christ Jesus" (Philippians 4:6–7).

# Faith or Denial?

## Denial Often Masquerades as Faith

A. J. was reassuring Bubba: "Don't worry about it. There always seems to be enough cookies, no matter how many we eat."

This was a recurring concern with Bubba and others. And it wasn't easily alleviated.

"How can I be sure?" Bubba wondered.

"Well, I don't know," A. J. said, "but my daddy said that everything seems to always just work out."

Ryan overheard this. "I know the real reason why there'll be enough cookies," he stated. "My mom brings them, and she always *knows* what we need."

Ryan had faith. But his faith wasn't in a plentiful supply of cookies; his faith was simply in Miss Marla, his mom, the one who always provided those cookies.

## Faith in What or Whom?

One of the earliest survival mechanisms I learned was denial. Through my early years of life, I strapped on a pair of rose-colored glasses called optimism and waltzed through life denying that there was anything bad happening to me or around me.

Being a victim of sexual abuse outside my home, I coped by denying the festering wounds, and by focusing on only good things. It was denial masquerading as faith. I was truly putting my faith in what I couldn't admit had happened and in what I hoped would happen in my future to make me happy.

But the recognition of my own sin awakened in me the great need of a Savior. I needed Someone to rescue me and give me a new life. Yet that same recognition of my sin led me to the sobering need to forgive the sins committed against me. I could no longer live in denial of what I'd done or what others had done to me.

God's light exposed all. To truly forgive a sin, you must call out what it truly is in light of the great evil that has been done.

Abortion isn't just a "solution;" it's murder. Sexual abuse isn't just an assault; it's the robbing of one's identity.

Once I was able to come face-to-face with the true nature of the evil committed against me, I was in the position to forgive. Then, in the light of Jesus' command to forgive one another, and in the power He alone can give, I was able to forgive those who had sinned against me.

My faith is now in Him who is able to make all things work for good toward those who love Him and are called to His purposes.

No longer do I live in the bondage of unforgiveness or the false sense of security that denial promises.

# Which Is Better, Giving or Receiving?

## "Exchanging Gifts" Is an Oxymoron

Everyone was so excited about our Christmas in July.

"Wow," Buck exclaimed. "I'll get two presents this year! I don't know who thought this one up, but I think I'm going to really like it!"

But Eric hung his head. He was sneaking through the crowded room, making eye contact with no one. His hands were in his pockets. He hadn't brought a present, which obviously meant he wasn't going to get any.

Meanwhile Ryan had brought two presents. I guess he expected to get more that way.

I had brought one, but I truly hoped what I received would be a lot nicer than what I'd brought, because I'd spent as little as possible on it. My philosophy was to give a little in exchange for a lot.

Miss Marla soon called everyone together to start the Christmas in July party. As she spoke, it slowly dawned on me that these presents weren't even for us! We had brought them to be sent overseas to some kids in a place I'd never heard of. *Myanmar?* I realized I didn't stand a chance of anyone there sending me something in return.

Buck looked as sad as I was. Eric looked relieved.

The only one smiling—as though he already knew the punch line—was Ryan. He truly seemed happy that he was giving two gifts and getting none.

Some things are truly outside this world.

## Giving and Living

Giving is a sticky subject. If you give with the expectation of receiving something from the receiver, then is it truly a gift?

I love the thought that selfless giving means providing something for someone who has absolutely no way to pay you back. But I've often given the right gift to the right person for the wrong reason. It might have been the desire to be praised or noticed or thought well of; or it could have been any number of other self-serving reasons. Do I get credit for such a gift?

I've given in the past with only a small expectation of a returned favor. I've even *not* given when the right thing to do would have been to give. At times I've given—from my heart—the right gift to the right person, only to see that gift squandered or rejected by the receiver. I've also given the wrong gift to the right person for the right reason and ended up harming that person. I've given money to an addicted mother to buy food for her kids, but she spent it on drugs.

Yes, giving is great—but hard to do well. Yet it is the joy of life.

I think *giving* is just another way to spell *living*. As I give,

I become less like the Dead Sea—void of life, always receiving, never giving out. By giving, I become more like a moving stream of living water, constantly being refreshed, renewed, and reformed and giving *life*.

I believe that paying back is not a gift, but paying forward is. And Jesus taught us clearly to pay it forward, for there's a storehouse in heaven waiting for us when we arrive.

I can't wait to see all the people in heaven who touched my life with their giving. Even more, I long to see all those who I was able to touch by just paying forward what God had given me to spend, in terms of my time, my talents, or my treasure.

Oh, what a day that will be!

# Where is Everybody Now?

## *Love the Ones You're with Later, Too*

Wow! What an amazing week! I had never dreamed that all these people I never knew before could be so cool.

From Hyper Eric, Pretty Emily, Ol' Man Ryan, Buddy Buck, Dark-Eyed Natasha, Cornrow Keisha, Big A. J., and Frogboy Timmy to Sweet Miss Marla, I now had the world's greatest friends.

Of course, I could say that Jesus was my best friend, even though I had no idea at the time what that really meant.

Back then, I thought time had frozen and would always be the way it was then, and my new friends would always stay close.

The next week, I was back in school, and I would pass a few of my new friends in the hall or see them standing by their bus, and we sensed a kindred bond. Sooner, rather than later, however, it faded.

Still, there were two who would walk with me throughout my life: Jesus and Buck.

Yeah … it seemed that in the times of darkness when I was groping my way through, Buck would show up and reveal Jesus's love for me. He's the only guy I've ever known who would take a bullet for me, who esteemed my life greater than his.

As for Jesus, He never left. At times I would look high and low, right and left, until one day I realized—He'd been living out His life through me! He never left me and never would leave me. His love is forever.

## Designed for Relationships

No matter how hard I try, it's so hard to maintain friendships without proximity. Looking back, I see the huge number of friends I've known in school from first grade on through pharmacy school, and all the friends I've made through work and business over the years, plus all the relationships I've developed in church and other gatherings of believers. I recognize how each of those relationships somehow enriched my life.

But there's never a substitute for being with someone on a consistent, ongoing basis.

God designed us for relationships in order to give and receive His love. That is done through contact. Just like an unplugged lamp doesn't give light, an unplugged relationship doesn't give life. We must make an effort to be in contact to give—and thus receive.

I still have a few friends who, regardless of the time between meeting or calling each other, it's as though we were never apart. But this happens only with contact.

My relationship with Christ is the same. Without an ongoing, conscious conversation with Him, my life becomes less about Him and others and more about me. When this happens, I can literally feel my energy seeping away as I'm trying to get my needs met outside of Him.

So loving is more than just an emotion; it's a deliberate effort of desiring to give to others.

In the riches of the grace of Jesus Christ, may you experience from now on a lifetime of true giving, true living, and true loving.

Mark B. Weaver is a graduate of the University of Kentucky and operates a financial planning practice that specializes in charitable estate planning. He serves on the board of elders for One Life Church Planting Network as well as on the board of other nonprofits. He is passionate about the concept of Transformational Generosity, generosity that changes both the giver and receiver, and speaks regularly on this subject. He currently resides in Henderson, Kentucky with his wife. He has two sons, one daughter-in-law, and two beautiful granddaughters.

Ben Wade is an award-winning freelance artist whose work has appeared in multiple books, album covers, newspapers, advertisements, etc. See his work at benwade93.crevado.com, follow him on Instagram at @kungfu_benny93, and contact him at benwade93@gmail.com.

CPSIA information can be obtained
at www.ICGtesting.com
Printed in the USA
LVHW111132211218
601293LV00001B/1/P